The Joy of Marriage

Poems for People in Love

Selected by Barbara Kunz Loots

Hallmark Editions

The publisher wishes to thank those who have given their kind permission to reprint material included in this book. Every effort has been made to give proper acknowledgments. Any omissions or errors are deeply regretted, and the publisher, upon notification, will be pleased to make necessary corrections in subsequent editions.

Acknowledgments: "Spectrum" by Maureen Cannon reprinted by permission from *Modern Bride* (December, 1970-January, 1971 issue). Copyright © 1970 by Maureen Cannon. "Wedding Day" by Maureen Cannon reprinted by permission from *Modern Bride* (August-September, 1970 issue). Copyright © 1970 by Ziff-Davis Publishing Company. "Most Like an Arch This Marriage" from *I Marry You* by John Ciardi. Copyright 1958 by Rutgers, The State University. Reprinted by permission of the author. Excerpt from *The White Cliffs* by Alice Duer Miller. Copyright 1940 by Alice Duer Miller; renewed 1967. Reprinted by permission of Coward, McCann & Geoghegan, Inc., Laurence Pollinger Limited, and the Estate of the late Alice Duer Miller. "To Be With You" from *The Poems of Max Ehrmann.* Copyright 1948 by Bertha K. Ehrmann. Reprinted by permission of Crescendo Publishers. "Eliena" from *Poems of Five Decades* by Max Eastman. Copyright 1954 by Max Eastman. Reprinted by permission of Mrs. Max Eastman. "Home Poem" by Maxine Lewis reprinted by permission of *Family Circle* Magazine. Copyright © 1972 by The Family Circle, Inc. "Your Day and Night" by Archibald Rutledge from the February, 1970 issue of *Good Housekeeping* Magazine. © 1970 by the Hearst Corporation. Reprinted by permission of *Good Housekeeping* Magazine and Irvine H. Rutledge. Chapter II from *The Song of Songs* by Solomon, taken from *The Holy Scriptures.* Copyrighted by The Jewish Society of America and used through the courtesy of The Jewish Publication Society of America. "Marriage Is a Place" by Deborah Roth from the January, 1975 issue of *Ladies' Home Journal.* © January, 1951, Downe Publishing, Inc. Reprinted with permission of Ladies' Home Journal. "Unity" from *Collected Poems,* Volume 2 by Alfred Noyes. Copyright 1913 by Frederick A. Stokes Company. Copyright 1906, 1909, renewed 1934, 1937, 1941 by Alfred Noyes. Reprinted by permission of J. B. Lippincott Company and Hugh Noyes, Esq. "Except My Love" reprinted with permission of Macmillan Publishing Co., Inc. from *Country Poems* by Elizabeth Coatsworth. Copyright 1931, 1933, 1934, 1935, 1936, 1938, 1942 by Elizabeth Coatsworth Beston. "To-night" reprinted with permission of Macmillan Publishing Co., Inc. from *Collected Poems* by Sara Teasdale. Copyright 1917 by Macmillan Publishing Co., Inc., renewed 1945 by Mamie T. Wheless. "Brown Penny" from *Collected Poems* by William Butler Yeats. Copyright 1912 by Macmillan Publishing Co., Inc., renewed 1940 by Bertha Georgie Yeats. Reprinted by permission of Macmillan Publishing Co., Inc., A. P. Watt & Son, M. B. Yeats, Miss Anne Yeats and Macmillan of London & Basingstoke. "When You Are Old" from *Collected Poems* by William Butler Yeats. Copyright 1906 by Macmillan Publishing Co., Inc., renewed 1934 by William Butler Yeats. Reprinted with permission of Macmillan Publishing Co., Inc., A. P. Watt & Son, M. B. Yeats, Miss Anne Yeats and Macmillan of London & Basingstoke. "A Decade" by Amy Lowell from *The Complete Poetical Works of Amy Lowell.* Reprinted by permission of the publisher, Houghton Mifflin Company. Excerpts from "Pleasant Song I" and "Pleasant Song II" from *Love Poems of Ancient Egypt* by Ezra Pound and Noel Stock. Copyright © 1962 by Noel Stock. Reprinted by permission of New Directions Publishing Corporation. "The Quarrel" from *Collected Poems* by Conrad Aiken. Copyright © 1953, 1970 by Conrad Aiken. Reprinted by permission of Oxford University Press, Inc. "Even" from *The Unicorn and Other Poems* by Anne Morrow Lindbergh. Copyright © 1956 by Anne Morrow Lindbergh. Reprinted by permission of Pantheon Books, a Division of Random House, Inc. "They Call Her Blessed" from Proverbs 31 from the Revised Standard Version of the Bible, copyrighted 1946, 1952, © 1971, 1973. Reprinted by permission of the National Council of the Churches of Christ.

© 1976, Hallmark Cards, Inc., Kansas City, Missouri.
Printed in the United States of America.
Library of Congress Catalog Card Number: 75-13017.
Standard Book Number: 87529-456-1.

The Joy of Marriage

Wedding Day

Wish upon a wisdom-star,
    Savor laughter.
Be exactly as you are
    Ever after.
And the bounties it can bring —
    Loving, living —
Rest upon one special thing:
    Giving.

Maureen Cannon

Love Song

Come walk with me
As twilight falls
And crimson splashes in the sky;
In shadowed pathways,
You and I
Can walk and dream.

And high upon some windblown cliff
Which overlooks the sea,
Come watch with me
The restive waves
That spill upon the sand...
Come closer, Love,
Give me your hand.

And as the sun's last rays
Take flight,
And evening melts into the night,
Keep vigil here
Beneath the stars
Which shimmer on the shore...
Then kiss me, Dear,
Once more, once more...

Locked in your arms,
My being sings,
And every dream that I have known
Comes true, for
I am yours alone.

Katherine Nelson Davis

True Love

True love is but a humble, low-born thing,
And hath its food served up in earthenware;
It is a thing to walk with, hand in hand,
Through the everydayness of this work-day world,
Baring its tender feet to every roughness,
Yet letting not one heart-beat go astray
From beauty's law of plainness and content —
A simple, fireside thing, whose quiet smile
Can warm earth's poorest hovel to a home.

James Russell Lowell

7 A.M.

The first time you saw
    my early-morning face,
    rumpled, wrinkled, whiskered,
    I thought the whole thing was over...
    but then you kissed me,
    soft as sun through fog,
    and I knew that the whole thing
    had just begun.

Kenneth Holt

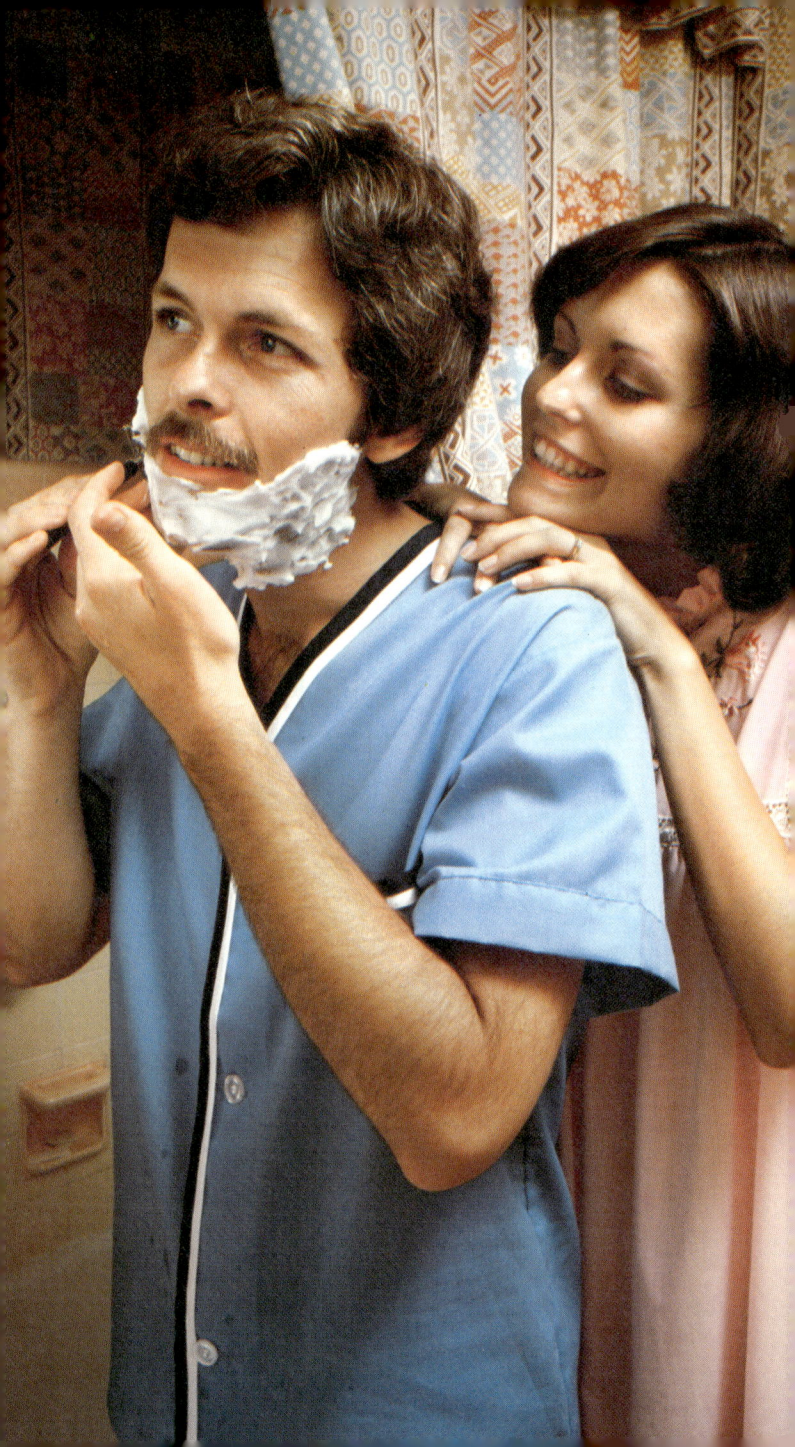

To Be With You

To be with you this evening,
                rarest of the evenings all,
And listen to the whispering leaves
                and to the night bird's call,
The silvery moonlight on your face —
To be with you in some still place.

To be with you somewhere
                within this evening's mystic shade,
To hear your plans and hopes
                and tell you mine, all unafraid
That you'd forget to hold them dear,
When I'm away and you're not here.

To be somewhere alone with you
                and watch the myriad stars,
Far golden worlds beyond the noisy earth's
                unkindly jars,
As quietly they sail night's sea
Above the world and you and me.

Max Ehrmann

A Decade

When you came,
      you were like red wine and honey,
And the taste of you
      burnt my mouth with its sweetness.
Now you are like morning bread,
Smooth and pleasant.
I hardly taste you at all, for I know your savor;
But I am completely nourished.

Amy Lowell

Eliena

Nimble with laughter, loving to be,
Courage quick and as quick a skill,
Pride that contains humility,
Love that adoring is thinking still —
Most men love in a girl some star,
I love you for the things you are.

Max Eastman

from The White Cliffs

Young and in love — how magical the phrase!
How magical the fact! Who has not yearned
Over young lovers when to their amaze
They fall in love, and find their love returned,
And the lights brighten, and their eyes are clear
To see God's image in their common clay.
Is it the music of the spheres they hear?
Is it the prelude to that noble play
The drama of Joined Lives?

Alice Duer Miller

Spring Song

The air was full of sun and birds,
    The fresh air sparkled clearly.
Remembrance wakened in my heart
    And I knew I loved her dearly.

The fallows and the leafless trees
    And all my spirit tingled.
My earliest thought of love, and Spring's
    First puff of perfume mingled.

In my still heart the thoughts awoke,
    Came lone by lone together —
Say, birds and Sun and Spring, is Love
    A mere affair of weather?

Robert Louis Stevenson

Brown Penny

I whispered, "I am too young."
And then, "I am old enough";
Wherefore I threw a penny
To find out if I might love.
"Go and love, go and love, young man,
If the lady be young and fair."
Ah, penny, brown penny, brown penny,
I am looped in the loops of her hair.
O love is the crooked thing,
There is nobody wise enough
To find out all that is in it,
For he would be thinking of love
Till the stars had run away,
And the shadows eaten the moon.
Ah, penny, brown penny, brown penny,
One cannot begin it too soon.

William Butler Yeats

To Love You

To love you
   is to love the trees,
   is to love the warm
   and gentle breeze,
   is to love the world I see...
To love you
   is to love the days,
   is to love the morning's
   warming rays
   and the night's tranquility...
To love you
   is to love to live,
   is to love to share
   and care and give,
   and it's wanting to be me...
To love you.

Mary Alice Loberg

from The Song of Songs

Hark! my beloved! behold, he cometh,
Leaping upon the mountains,
                skipping upon the hills.
My beloved is like a gazelle or a young hart;
Behold, he standeth behind our wall,
He looketh in through the windows,
He peereth through the lattice.
My beloved spoke, and said unto me:
"Rise up, my love, my fair one, and come away.
For, lo, the winter is past,
The rain is over and gone;
The flowers appear on the earth;
The time of singing is come,
And the voice of the turtledove
                is heard in our land...."

Solomon

A Blessing for Marriage

May your house be strong of beam,
Firm of wall and rafter,
Built with timber of a dream,
Girded well with laughter.
May it have a winding stair
With a lover's landing,
Windows to let in the air
And light of understanding.
May it have a roof of faith
For every change of weather,
And love upon the hearth to warm
All your years together.

Esther York Burkholder

Love Is

Sunlight dancing
   in the heart,
Speaking in silences,
Joy at your fingertips,
Secret delights
   of discoveries shared,
Starshine sparkling
   in the mind,
A smile on your soul.

Barbara Plumb

They Call Her Blessed

A good wife who can find?
    She is far more precious than jewels.
The heart of her husband trusts in her,
    and he will have no lack of gain.
She does him good, and not harm,
    all the days of her life....
Strength and dignity are her clothing,
    and she laughs at the time to come.
She opens her mouth with wisdom,
    and the teaching of kindness is on her tongue.
She looks well to the ways of her household,
    and does not eat the bread of idleness.
Her children rise up and call her blessed;
    her husband also, and he praises her.

from Proverbs 31

Your Love to Me

Your love to me
Is as the beat
Of wings against the sky —
The surge of fire
Through forest —
A field where
Spring passed by.
Your love to me
Is as the pulse
Of sea in hurricane —
Thunder heeled on lightning,
Sunshaft after rain.
Ever changing,
Ever constant,
Old as life,
And yet as new —
Your love to me is the magic
And the wonder
That is you.

Mary R. Hurley

Except My Love

What can I give you worth your loneliness?
What can I say that silence has not said?
The solitary wanderer hears a music
Vast as the winds, deep as the ocean's tread.

The solitary wanderer walks through dewfall,
For him each star stirs like a crystal dove —
What have I to exchange for your aloneness
Except my love?

Elizabeth Coatsworth

Even —

Him that I love I wish to be
Free:

Free as the bare top twigs of tree,
Pushed up out of the fight
Of branches, struggling for the light,
Clear of the darkening pall,
Where shadows fall —
Open to the golden eye
Of sky;

Free as a gull
Alone upon a single shaft of air,
Invisible there,
Where
No man can touch,
No shout can reach,
Meet
No stare;

Free as a spear
Of grass,
Lost in the green
Anonymity
Of a thousand seen
Piercing, row on row;
The crust of earth,
With mirth,
Through to the blue,
Sharing the sun
Although,
Circled, each one,
In his cool sphere
Of dew.

Him that I love, I wish to be
Free —
Even from me.

Anne Morrow Lindbergh

Most Like an Arch This Marriage

Most like an arch — an entrance that upholds
and shores the stone-crush up the air like lace.
Mass made idea, and idea held in place.
A lock in time. Inside half-heaven unfolds.

Most like an arch — two weaknesses that lean
into a strength. Two fallings become firm.
Two joined abeyances become a term
naming the fact that teaches fact to mean.

Not quite that? Not much less. World as it is,
what's strong and separate falters. All I do
at piling stone on stone apart from you
is roofless around nothing. Till we kiss

I am no more than upright and unset.
It is by falling in and in we make
the all-bearing point, for one another's sake,
in faultless failing, raised by our own weight.

John Ciardi

Home Poem

Where love finds a place,
Beautiful things are...
Like going upstairs together,
Like going down alone in the night barefoot
    to query the lock.
Like watching the weather
    Rain stinging the windows
    Snow clinging to the panes
    Wind singing.
    (Love is lovely when it rains.)
Like sitting across from each other
    and not being cross.
Like not getting up in the morning.
    No loss!
    (Except time's little cry from the clock.)
Like his finding her earring
    And her finding his sock.
It's a total of both tied up in a bundle of walls.
An echo chamber of selves connected by halls.

Maxine Lewis

The Days of Your Togetherness

Now you will feel no rain,
    for each of you will be shelter to the other.
Now you will feel no cold,
    for each of you will be warmth to the other.
Now there is no more loneliness,
    for each of you will be companion to the other.
Now you are two bodies,
    but there is only one life before you.
Go now to your dwelling place,
    to enter into the days of your togetherness,
And may your days be good
    and long upon the earth.

from an Apache ceremony

The Golden Circle of Love

Like two golden wedding rings,
    two circles linked to one another,
        circles never ending or beginning —
so the golden circles of your years
    are linked together in love
        that cannot break
            and will not sever,
for the beautiful gold of true love
    will shine on forever.

Author Unknown

Spectrum

Color of dusk, this room at five o'clock,
Color of waiting.... Suddenly the rhythm
Falters, begins to quicken as the lock
Turns and he enters, fills the room, brings with him
Color of my contentment. The hour, surmounted,
Completes itself — color of blessings, counted.

Maureen Cannon

A Dedication

In dawn's wakening smile,
   in bright new promises of morning,
      I have seen your eyes...
In music of midday,
   in sweet soaring vibrancy of earthsongs,
      I have heard your voice...
In evening's warm caress,
   in sheltering closeness of sunset,
      I have felt your touch...
All things beautiful in my world
   have breathed the magic,
      the mystery, the miracle of you...
I have loved you this day.

Edward Cunningham

Love Poems of Ancient Egypt

...Knowing for certain that you love me
I nestle at your side.

My heart is sure that among all
Men you are the main one for me.

The whole world shines.
I wish we could go on sleeping together,
Like this, to the end of eternity.

...Tranquil our paths
When your hand rests on mine in joy.

Your voice gives life, like nectar.

To see you is more than food or drink.

Marriage Is a Place

How unlike we are
You a laughing child of May
Springtime green, Irish heart, an emerald's strength
And I, October's child
Autumn's fruit, wine red, an opal's hope
As different, we two, as Spring and Fall
Yet weighed on Nature's scales we balance one another
As seasons balance out the year.

As you, lover of fact and footnote, have taught me
One and one are never one, but two
So you and I are separate and distinct
Nor tied, nor locked together, but apart
Only there in that special place
Where our worlds combine as circles intersect
To share a common space
There is where you and I become us
In a place we share called Marriage.

Deborah Roth

To-night

The moon is a curving flower of gold,
    The sky is still and blue;
The moon was made for the sky to hold,
    And I for you.

The moon is a flower without a stem,
    The sky is luminous;
Eternity was made for them,
    To-night for us.

Sara Teasdale

Love's Garden

Marriage opens the gate
   to love's gentle garden.
Their promise made, the bride and groom
   rush in to greet life,
      lying splendid before them.
Together they discover
   the rich perfume
      and melodious song of love;
They share nature's secrets,
   her happiness,
   and standing beneath a willow...
      they kiss.

Tina Hacker

The Quarrel

Suddenly, after the quarrel, while we waited,
Disheartened, silent,
                with downcast looks, nor stirred
Eyelid nor finger, hopeless both, yet hoping
Against all hope to unsay the sundering word:

While the room's stillness deepened,
                            deepened about us,
And each of us crept his thought's way to discover
How, with as little sound as the fall of a leaf,
The shadow had fallen,
                and lover quarrelled with lover;

And while, in the quiet, I marvelled — alas, alas —
At your deep beauty, your tragic beauty, torn
As the pale flower is torn by the wanton sparrow —
This beauty, pitied and loved, and now forsworn;

It was then,
        when the instant darkened to its darkest, —
When faith was lost with hope,
                              and the rain conspired
To strike its gay arpeggios against our heartstrings, —
When love no longer dared, and scarcely desired:

It was then that suddenly, in the neighbor's room,
The music started: that brave quartette of strings
Breaking out of the stillness, as out of our stillness,
Like the indomitable heart of life that sings

When all is lost; and startled from our sorrow,
Tranced from our grief by the diviner grief,
We raised remembering eyes, each looked at other,
Blinded with tears of joy; and another leaf

Fell silently as that first; and in the instant
The shadow had gone, our quarrel became absurd;
And we rose, to the angelic voices of the music,
And I touched your hand,
                and we kissed, without a word.

Conrad Aiken

Your Day and Night

O well I love the Day of you,
The radiant sunlit way of you,
The laughter lithe and gay of you,
The morning and the May of you,
Your azure with its lark.

But O the glimmering Night of you,
The stealing wild starlight of you,
The mystery and sleep of you,
The shadows and the deep of you,
The secrecy and hush of you,
The hidden bloom and blush of you,
The fragrance in the dark!

Archibald Rutledge

When You Are Old

When you are old and gray and full of sleep,
And nodding by the fire, take down this book,
And slowly read, and dream of the soft look
Your eyes had once, and of their shadows deep;

How many loved your moments of glad grace,
And loved your beauty with love false or true;
But one man loved the pilgrim soul in you,
And loved the sorrows of your changing face.

And bending down beside the glowing bars,
Murmur, a little sadly, how love fled
And paced upon the mountains overhead
And hid his face amid a crowd of stars.

William Butler Yeats

I Wish I Could Remember That First Day

I wish I could remember that first day,
First hour, first moment of your meeting me,
If bright or dim the season, it might be
Summer or winter for aught I can say;
So unrecorded did it slip away,
So blind was I to see and to foresee,
So dull to mark the budding of my tree
That would not blossom yet for many a May.
If only I could recollect it, such
A day of days! I let it come and go
As traceless as a thaw of bygone snow;
It seemed to mean so little, meant so much;
If only now I could recall that touch,
First touch of hand in hand — did one but know!

Christina Rossetti

Unity

Heart of my heart, the world is young:
Love lies hidden in every rose,
Every song that the skylark sung
Once, we thought, must come to a close:
Now we know the spirit of song,
Song that is merged in the chant of the whole,
Hand in hand as we wander along,
What should we doubt of the years that roll?

Heart of my heart, we cannot die!
Love triumphant in flower and tree,
Every life that laughs at the sky
Tells us nothing can cease to be;
One, we are one with a song today,
One with the clover that scents the world,
One with the Unknown, far away,
One with the stars, when earth grows old.

Heart of my heart, we are one with the wind.
One with the clouds that are whirled o'er the lea,
One in many O broken and blind,
One as the waves are at one with the sea!
Ay! when life seems scattered apart,
Darkens, ends as a tale that is told,
One, we are one, O heart of my heart,
One, still one, while the world grows old.

Alfred Noyes

Set in Perpetua, a typeface
designed by Eric Gill, first appearing in 1925.
Printed on Crown Royale Book paper.
Designed by Myron McVay.